A LOONIE FOR LUCK

FOREWORD BY WAYNE GRETZKY

A LOONIE FOR LUCK

BY ROY MacGREGOR

Illustrations by Bill Slavin

M&S

National Library of Canada Cataloguing in Publication

MacGregor, Roy, 1948–
    A loonie for luck / Roy MacGregor ; foreword by Wayne Gretzky ; illustrated by Bill Slavin.

ISBN 0-7710-5480-7

    1. Winter Olympic Games (19th : 2002 : Salt Lake City, Utah)
2. Hockey — Canda — History — 21st century. I. Title.

GV848.4.C3M32 2002   796.962'66   C2002-903541-4

Tim Hortons coffee cup design and logo reproduced on page 18 with permission of Tim Hortons, operated by the TDL Group Ltd.

We acknowledge the financial support of the Government of Canada through the Book Publishing Industry Development Program for our publishing activities. We further acknowledge the support of the Canada Council for the Arts and the Ontario Arts Council for our publishing program.

Typeset in Janson by Sharon Foster
Printed and bound in Canada

McClelland & Stewart Ltd.
The Canadian Publishers
481 University Avenue
Toronto, Ontario
M5G 2E9
www.mcclelland.com

1 2 3 4 5   06 05 04 03 02

Foreword

THIS IS a story about magic.

I can still remember walking up to Trent Evans that Sunday afternoon in Salt Lake City right after Team Canada had won the men's gold medal – Canada's second hockey gold medal in three days. I put an arm around his shoulder and whispered in his ear, "You're going to be a legend."

The room was already filled with players who are hockey legends, like Mario Lemieux and Steve Yzerman and Joe Sakic, and players who one day will be, like Jarome Iginla and Martin Brodeur, and yet here was Trent Evans, a perfectly average guy, a Zamboni driver from Edmonton – and how much more Canadian can you get than *that*? – who had just become a true hero in his own right.

The guy who hid the loonie at centre ice.

Before we even left Salt Lake City, the story of that loonie had become folklore in the world of hockey. Right from the moment I was told it was there, I believed that coin stood for just how much Canadians care about our game. It wasn't so much about good luck – though we were glad to have any help we could get – as it was about the country as a whole being a part of this wonderful Olympic experience, thanks to Trent Evans.

I knew at once where that coin belonged. Trent was originally going to keep it for his own kids, then he figured he should give it to me as a memento. But that didn't feel right to me, just as it hadn't felt right to him to hang on to it for himself.

"This loonie's for *all* Canadians," I told him. "It belongs in the Hockey Hall of Fame."

I wanted young Canadians to see it, and touch it, and know about it, and maybe understand just a little bit better how deeply the game matters to this country.

Those two victories in Salt Lake did a lot of good things for Canada. They showed us that the Canadian Hockey Association and minor-league coaches everywhere are doing a lot of things right. We're not saying Canadian hockey is perfect, and we don't say it can't be improved, but we *are* saying that the birthplace of hockey is still the best place for hockey, right from atom house league to the National Hockey League, right from the best players in the world to the best ice makers in the world, like Edmonton's Trent Evans.

I wanted the loonie to go to the Hall of Fame. And I wanted this story told so that people would never forget that those gold medals were for the whole country, not just the players. That's why I suggested to Trent that we talk to Roy MacGregor about turning his story into a book. Roy and I once worked together on a newspaper column in my first year after retirement, and both my two boys and Trent's two boys are, like so many hockey-mad youngsters, huge fans of Roy's Screech Owls hockey mystery series, so he was the one we wanted to tell this great story in a way that fans of all ages could know what it was like to be in Salt Lake City that February and know how a little piece of Canada came to be buried at centre ice.

Trent could not, really, have picked a better place to put that loonie. It was perfect.

We had put the team together with speed and skill in mind, and we needed not just good ice, we needed *true* ice – ice that passers like Mario could use without having to worry about the puck wobbling and skipping, ice that our mobile defence could be sure of if they wanted to gamble. We wanted ice that the best players in the world could work with. If we had just put together a team consisting of the very best players Canada has, then we owed it to them to make sure the ice in Salt Lake was as good as it gets.

To me, that meant Edmonton ice.

The National Hockey League had long known that the Edmonton Oilers play on the best ice surface in the world – fast, true ice that even the visiting players love – and several years back the league had recognized that fact by getting Edmonton's Dan Craig to become the NHL's ice consultant. The guys in Edmonton made the best ice in the eighties, when I played there, and they still make the best ice. They have it down to a science. In fact, they *are* the science.

And no one, believe me, makes better ice than Trent Evans.

I've known that for more than twenty years. I can still remember coming early to a practice at the old Northlands Coliseum and seeing Paul Coffey, in full equipment, already out on the ice with Trent. The two of them were down on their hands and knees so low it looked like their noses were frozen to the ice. But they weren't stuck; they were checking it out. Or, more likely, just admiring Trent's handiwork.

Now, you have to understand one thing about Paul Coffey: he's an absolute fanatic about things like his skates and rink ice. I don't think any player in the history of the game has ever known more, or studied more, about such matters as how your blades are sharpened and rockered or what's the best kind of ice to skate on. I'd also have to say that no player in the history of the game has ever skated better than Paul. We used to say he was the only player anybody had ever seen who could actually *pick up speed* while he was coasting. So if Paul approved of what you were doing, you were doing it right.

And Paul Coffey was a Trent Evans fan. A huge fan.

You can well imagine my delight, then, when I found out Trent would be one of the ice makers at Salt Lake City's E Center, where we intended to be playing in the gold medal game on Sunday afternoon, February 24, 2002.

I got there on Friday, February 8, in time for the opening ceremonies, and on Saturday morning I went out to the E Center to check out the facilities. I wanted to make sure that the locker room assigned to Team Canada was going to be set up exactly right. We'd done a great deal of thinking about how we wanted it done, always considering how we might inspire the players and keep them sharp and focused when they were dressing for games or even just resting between periods. I wanted the pennants up from all the Olympic championships Canada had ever won in hockey, and I wanted pictures of those old teams posted on the walls so the players would look at them as they walked out of the dressing room toward the ice surface. The final photograph I wanted them to see was the one of the 1952 Edmonton Mercurys, the last Canadian team to win Olympic gold in hockey.

As chance would have it, the gold medal game in Salt Lake City was scheduled to be played fifty years *to the day* from when the Mercurys had won in Oslo. And I wanted to do everything within my power as executive director of the team to make sure our players were aware of what the Mercs had done and how very long it had been between Olympic gold medals for the country that had given hockey to the world.

As I kept saying in Salt Lake, fifty years is a long time to be the kings of hockey without wearing the crown.

I also wanted to make sure that Mario Lemieux, our captain, had his seat in the dressing room set up exactly right. I thought Mario should sit in a place where he would be able to see the entire room and, more importantly, every player could see him. I wanted the players to have to look Mario in the eyes between periods, because I was very aware what these games meant to Mario, how determined he was to bring back the gold. He was coming in with a bad hip that should have kept him from playing, but he was absolutely determined to play. And not only play, but win. It was like he was on a *mission* – and I wanted to do whatever I could to ensure he went back home with that mission accomplished.

I was just finishing up in the dressing room with my Team Canada assistants, Kevin Lowe and Steve Tambellini, when Trent Evans came along. Kevin's the general manager of the Oilers, so he and Trent see each other pretty well every day, but I hadn't run into Trent for a while. We were catching up when he said he had something to show us.

We had no idea what was up, but the three of us followed Trent out onto the ice. There was hardly anyone else around – the rink was empty but for a few workers. He took us right to centre ice and pointed down.

We couldn't see a thing, to tell the truth. Maybe a hint of yellow or something. I had no idea what he was up to.

"There's a Canadian loonie buried down there," Trent said. "And nobody knows about it. I hid it there for you guys – for luck."

I looked again. I couldn't believe it. I couldn't really see it either, so I had to take him at his word. I started to giggle, it seemed like such a crazy thing to do. But *neat* – a beautiful, truly Canadian touch.

"I love it," I told him. "But whatever you do, don't tell anybody."

Soon, however, it seemed like every Canadian in Salt Lake City knew the secret. There were a few times, in fact, when I was convinced it wouldn't survive – especially when several of the women started *kissing* the ice over the loonie after they'd won their gold and we still had two games left to play!

Foreword

But it did survive, and three days after the women's victory, Trent's little secret became the great surprise of the Olympic hockey tournament, a magical story that is now treasured by those directly involved and by the millions of Canadians who cheered on their Olympic teams.

A nice portion of the royalties from *A Loonie for Luck* will be going to the Wayne Gretzky Foundation, a project I began after the Olympics to help make sure that North American kids without means can get the equipment they need to play hockey and join a minor hockey program that will let them become a part of the greatest game on earth.

The Canadian game.

Our game.

Wayne Gretzky
Los Angeles, July 2002

A LOONIE FOR LUCK

1

TRENT EVANS is a creature of habit. You want the day to go right, you start it right, and that means you begin at the local Tim Hortons, on Sherwood Park's Main Boulevard, with a large coffee, black, to go. You head out from there to the Yellowhead Highway, which takes you into Edmonton. The same route every time, the coffee finished exactly on arrival, and the day about to begin at the Skyreach Centre, where Trent Evans is in charge of what every player in the National Hockey League will tell you, without asking, is the finest ice surface in the world.

But this day was going to be different. Trent had been looking forward to it ever since an envelope had turned up five months earlier in the office mail, an envelope carrying the five linked circles of the Olympics logo and a Salt Lake City return address.

The letter inside was dated September 13, 2001. It was from the organizing committee for the Salt Lake City Olympic Winter Games of 2002, and it was signed by Nate Anderson, the committee's hockey coordinator. "Dear

Trent," the one-page letter began, "Mr. Dan Craig from NHL hockey operations has recommended you as one of the top ice technicians in North America. The Salt Lake Organizing Committee is pleased to request your services this February to assist in hosting the 2002 Olympic Winter Games."

Trent could hardly believe his luck. It would be a tough, gruelling schedule. All the organizing committee could offer was room and board, a volunteer uniform, and a small honorarium. He would be gone most of February, the longest he had ever been away from Laurel and their two boys, ten-year-old Justin and eight-year-old Jarret. But Laurel, when he phoned her, said it was a once-in-a-lifetime opportunity he should not pass up, and the boys were as hockey-mad as any Canadian youngsters. They could barely contain their excitement. Their father was going to the Winter Games, where Canada was hoping to win its first Olympic gold medal in hockey in fifty years – perhaps even *double* gold if, somehow, the men's team and women's team could accomplish what had been denied them four years earlier in Nagano, Japan.

Trent liked that thought. The thirty-five-year-old Calgary native had never been a great athlete: an average hockey player, a pretty fair golfer. But here he was, off to the *Olympics*.

In his own small way, he felt he, too, was representing his country, the land that had given the world the fastest team game ever known. The better the ice, the better their chances, Trent figured, and if the best ice in hockey was usually to be found in Edmonton, Alberta, Canada, then for a few weeks in February he would make sure it was also to be found in Salt Lake City, Utah. *Canadian* ice, for the Canadian game.

And now the big day had arrived. Trent Evans was on his way to Salt Lake City. But one little ritual didn't get forgotten: a hot coffee for the drive in to work, even if work this time was in another country. He drove around to the takeout window, handed over a five-dollar bill, collected his coffee, and pocketed his change.

Didn't count it, didn't even look at it.

He had, however, just pocketed a coin that would change his life.

2

THE DATE on the loonie Trent Evans had shoved into his pocket was 1987.

It was one of 205,405,000 dollar coins that were stamped by the Royal Canadian Mint in Winnipeg that very first year of production. They were produced at a rate of one million coins a day, each one exactly the same as the others. This particular coin was now fifteen years old, three-quarters of its "currency" life already spent. It came out of the Tim Hortons takeout window with no record of where it had travelled, no count of the number of parking meters or newspaper boxes or pop machines it had gone through, no mention of how many cash registers it had been in or, for that matter, how many piggy banks it had been taken from, nothing to say how many pockets it had known, what useful or useless items it had purchased, how many parents had handed it to how many children, how many times it had been lost, found, or merely forgotten on a dresser for months at a time.

That the loonie existed at all was due to an accident. The Canadian government had decided, in the mid-eighties, to retire the familiar green one-dollar bill and replace it with a new coin. The dollar coins would cost only twelve cents apiece to manufacture and would have twenty-six times the life span of the old dollar bill. The House of Commons committee that had recommended adoption of a dollar coin projected a saving of $175 million over the first twenty years alone.

Other countries, including the United States, had made similar attempts to replace paper money with coins, but the public did not always warm to metal money. And, at first, the Canadian effort appeared similarly doomed. The people were not particularly open to the idea, according to the polls, and there was angry debate in Parliament over the Royal Canadian Mint's intention to replace the traditional *voyageurs* design which had graced the little-used Canadian silver dollar since 1935. So much public pressure was applied, in fact, that the mint eventually decided to dump the intended new design and go back, instead, to the familiar fur traders paddling their birchbark canoe.

The coin was to be eleven-sided to help the visually impaired distinguish it from other coins. It was to be mostly nickel, with bronze plating, and would be a colour more in keeping, many thought, with a lowly penny than a dollar.

It would be minted in Winnipeg, where all Canadian coins are stamped. The dies with the new design, featuring the reborn *voyageurs*, were sent from Ottawa by courier to begin production.

Something happened, however, along the way. The dies never arrived. Those who were in charge of the coin that was supposed to save $175 million decided to save another $43.50

by having a local courier pick up the dies at the Winnipeg airport instead of using an armed security service. Someone did pick up the dies, but they were never seen again.

That was where the loonie was born. In a mad rush to replace the dies, as well as ensure that counterfeiters couldn't use the missing ones, a replacement design featuring the common loon – by Robert-Ralph Carmichael, one of the country's best-known wildlife artists – was rushed into production, and the poor *voyageurs* vanished into the wilderness of lost mail.

At first, Canadians didn't like the loon at all. With the Canadian dollar taking frequent hits, it was easy to joke about how *voyageurs* in canoes stay afloat while loons sink, even dive. But gradually, over time, people warmed to the new coins. They were handy, for one thing, and once kids and comics began calling the new coins "loonies," they had a catchy name that stuck, so much so that, years later, when the government decided to take the orange two-dollar bill out of circulation and replace it with a coin, the new coin automatically became the "*two*-nie."

Nineteen eighty-seven was also a big year for hockey. On the last day of May, the Edmonton Oilers, led by Wayne Gretzky, became the first expansion team to win three Stanley Cups.

In June, the amateur draft would contain one of the great hidden gems of all time when the Quebec Nordiques, using a selection acquired in an earlier deal with the Washington Capitals, used the fifteenth pick of the day to select a shy, skinny seventeen-year-old from Burnaby, B.C., named Joe Sakic.

That September, the Canada Cup was played, with the predicted showdown in the final between the powerful Soviet Union and a Team Canada that included Gretzky, Coffey, and a young francophone centre named Mario Lemieux, who was just beginning to come into his own with the Pittsburgh Penguins.

The two world powers met in a best-of-three final, each game decided by a 6-5 score.

The Soviets won the first match in Montreal. The loss, in overtime, was so dispiriting that many Canadian fans believed the Soviets would have little trouble winning one of the next two matches and laying claim to the trophy that, in the years before NHL players were freed up to play in the Olympics, was the best measure of world hockey supremacy.

But the Canadian players were not through. They came back in the second game, in Hamilton, to win 6-5, also in overtime, when Lemieux scored on a perfect set-up from Gretzky.

Then, in the third and final game, with only 1:26 remaining, Gretzky again sent Lemieux in on the Soviet goaltender, and Lemieux scored what is regarded as the second-greatest goal ever scored by a Canadian in international play, second only to Paul Henderson's legendary winning goal in the 1972 Summit Series.

It was that Canada Cup, people said, that saw Wayne Gretzky teach Mario Lemieux what winning was all about. Lemieux would go on to win two Stanley Cups with the Penguins before being forced into early retirement in 1997 by a bad back and a difficult, but successful, battle against cancer.

In the fifteen years since the loonie was born and the Canada Cup won in Hamilton, Mario Lemieux had not played again for Canada in international play. But now he was back, out of retirement and the obvious choice as captain of Wayne Gretzky's Team Canada.

Trent Evans couldn't have picked a more appropriate loonie if he'd searched through all 795,865,541 loonies that have been minted since that first year.

The year Mario Lemieux came true.

3

TRENT FLEW to Salt Lake City with Duncan Murie, another volunteer from Skyreach, and they were joined there by Mike Craig, of Kelowna, B.C., the son of Dan Craig, the NHL official in charge of the Olympic ice. All three Canadian ice makers would be working primarily at the E Center, the main rink, the only one of four not game-ready. They had one week to change all that.

Trent's first sight of the E Center was impressive – a modern, glassed-in structure with the snow-covered Wasatch Mountains rising behind – but he was far more concerned with what he saw inside. After the men had checked through the metal detectors and security searches that were everywhere at Salt Lake following the terrorist attacks the previous September in New York and Washington, they entered a building still in the process of being reconfigured to accommodate the larger international ice surface required by the Olympics. There was a new and wider concrete slab to form the floor of the rink, but little else was completed. Much of the protective glass still had to be installed, and there were no

markers to indicate where such critical elements as the faceoff circles or the complicated, multicoloured Olympic logos would be painted into the ice.

The first preliminary-round matches – Germany against Slovakia and France versus Switzerland – were scheduled for Saturday. The crew had only five working days to bring the rink and the ice to Olympic perfection.

Fifteen volunteers were on the ice-making crew, and the three Canadians among them considered themselves the "Edmonton Connection," in that Mike Craig's father had long been a main force behind the city's reputation for great ice and had taught all three of them the fine art of superior ice making.

The Edmonton connection at the games was extraordinary. Canada's last gold medal in Olympic hockey had been won fifty years earlier by the Edmonton Mercurys. The team at Salt Lake City had been put together by Wayne Gretzky, the executive director of Team Canada, who had won four Stanley Cups as an Edmonton Oiler and who held, when he retired, more than sixty NHL records. The team's assistant general manager was Kevin Lowe, also a former Oiler and the NHL team's current GM. Barrie Stafford, the longtime trainer and equipment manager for the Oilers, was there as a trainer; Ken Lowe was one of the equipment managers; Bill Tuele, the Oilers' public relations head, was handling media; and two young Oiler players, forward Ryan Smyth and defenceman Eric Brewer, were on the team.

Trent Evans was nervous, but it had nothing to do with how Team Canada would perform. Wearing his new green volunteer uniform, his credentials dangling from his neck, he looked around him that first morning on the job and wondered how they'd possibly get all their work done in time. None of the ice makers had ever worked with the kind of complicated logos the Olympics demanded. They also had to determine how everything, in the end, would square up on what was, essentially, a brand-new ice surface.

It took Trent a few moments to realize what it was that had made him so uneasy. There was a difference here, something that he had never dealt with before, and it was baffling him. All NHL rinks have a very clearly marked centre, a special plug screwed into the concrete that serves as an essential point of reference. The ice makers measure everything out from there; it ensures that all is kept in perfect order. From the centre plug, they lay out the twelve-inch blue faceoff circle and they also work a pivot that allows them to paint the centre ice circle. Everything begins at centre ice for ice makers, and spreads out from there.

Only there was no centre at the E Center!

Trent got to work, measuring out where centre ice should be, satisfying himself and the other ice makers that they had got it right. It wasn't easy, but the job was finally finished, various reference points around the floor had been established for the lines and faceoff circles to be painted later, and they were ready to begin the long and complicated process of making the ice.

With the cooling unit on, the ice makers first sprayed a fine mist over the new concrete slab to seal everything in. If they began by flooding, all the dirt and dust on the surface would simply float to the top and ruin the ice. First the fine mist, then a special white paint sprayed over the entire surface to set a colour base for the ice, then another mist spray.

Now they were ready to flood lightly until the ice was approximately one-eighth of an inch thick, at which point the difficult job of painting in the lines and logos could start.

Once that was done, the logos painted on the ice using stencils, there was one other detail to remember. With no blue faceoff circle as they had in NHL rinks, the referees would need some visible mark at centre ice to aim the puck at when they dropped it at the start of each game. Trent placed a cellphone call to Dan Craig to find out how he might mark the spot.

Craig was checking the ice in one of the two practice rinks.

"How did they mark it there?" Trent asked.

"We used a splotch of yellow paint," Craig answered.

"How big?"

"I don't know," Craig's voice crackled through the static. "Not big. About the size of a loonie."

Trent thanked Craig and put away his cellphone. He would have to get some paint, but first he wanted to mark the spot with something handy. He dug around in his change and came up with a dime, which he placed at exactly the right spot.

That night, back at the room they shared at Motel 6, Trent and Duncan sat talking about whether or not they'd make the deadline. Considerable progress had been made, but there was still a lot of work to do. And now they had to find a way to create a permanent mark at centre ice; once the flooding was complete and the ice was in use, skate marks would soon obscure the little dime.

An idea suddenly struck Trent. Dan Craig had suggested a yellow splotch of paint "about the size of a loonie." Only two Canadians could have had such a conversation on a cellphone and understood each other. No Canadian would ever call it a "one-dollar coin." The loonie – the Canadian dollar coin with Queen Elizabeth II on one side and the common loon on the other – was about as *Canadian* as you could get in Salt Lake City.

Trent got up, rooted around in his change, and came up with the loonie he'd picked up in his change the day before at Tim Hortons.

He held it up and looked at it. Dan had suggested "a splotch of yellow paint . . . about the size of a loonie."

Well, Trent thought, contemplating the gold-coloured coin, *why not a loonie?*

4

TRENT CAME by his little superstitions easily. He'd been working around the Edmonton rink for twenty years now, starting out as a "rink rat" at fifteen when he followed his older brother, Kevin, into a job offered by a Northlands worker who happened to live in the neighbourhood. Twenty years of being around the Edmonton Oilers would turn anyone into a believer in lucky charms and talismans and strange superstitions.

Led by three youngsters – Gretzky and Messier on forward, Paul Coffey on defence – the Oilers were the most promising team in hockey when Trent began flooding their ice. They were coached by Glen Sather, who had the good sense to give the youngsters their own head and let them be as creative as they wished. They had an exceptional young goaltender in Grant Fuhr, another promising young defenceman in Kevin Lowe and, at various times, a cast of character players that included Dave Semenko and Marty McSorley, the brilliant Kent Nilsson, and skaters the likes of Glenn

Anderson and Jari Kurri. They were the fastest team in hockey, and Sather insisted they have the best ice in hockey on which to work their magic. By the time the dynasty had had its full run, there were five Stanley Cup banners flying from the Northlands rafters.

They were also, by their own admission, perhaps the most superstitious hockey team ever to play together in a game renowned far beyond any other sport for its quirks and idiosyncrasies. Beards grown during the playoffs are only the tip of an iceberg of superstition.

Most fans will recall that dead octopus slapping down onto the ice in Detroit's Joe Louis Arena as the Red Wings and the Carolina Hurricanes played the final few minutes of the final game of the 2002 Stanley Cup. But few will know that the custom dates from 1952, when a local seafood merchant threw an octopus down from the stands and later claimed that its eight arms represented the eight victories necessary, in the age of the Original Six, to claim the Stanley Cup. No matter that it now takes sixteen wins; there being no sixteen-arm octopi, the standard eight-arm variety is still called upon in Detroit to observe the superstition.

The Philadelphia Flyers used to have Kate Smith sing "God Bless America" instead of the U.S. national anthem before games they absolutely had to win, and when Smith's belting soprano helped them to two Cups in the seventies, the song became so important to the team that even after the singer died in 1986 they continued to turn to her rendition during the playoffs – by playing a video recording on the scoreboard screen.

Such superstitions do not have to make sense. Flyers, and later New York Rangers, coach Fred Shero used to carry rosary beads during games, though he was not a Roman Catholic. Former Toronto Maple Leafs coach Red Kelly convinced the players they would perform better with "pyramid power" and put small pyramids beneath the bench. A previous Leafs coach, Punch Imlach, insisted on wearing a fedora though the games were played indoors, and once, after a pigeon had bombed his treasured hat while he walked to a game, which the Leafs then won, he refused to clean off the hat until the winning streak had come to an end.

Coaches, however, have nothing on the players. Psychologists who have studied the enduring power of superstition in sports have often speculated as to why the belief in charms and omens is so particularly strong in hockey. Some believe it is because the early players came from rural backgrounds and had little or no formal education. The tendency may then have endured because it became part of the culture of hockey even as the players became better educated, more urban, and more cosmopolitan as the Canadian game spread through the world.

For whatever reason, the players are, at times, fanatical about their good-luck charms. Hall-of-Famer Phil Esposito used to go into a rage if he happened to see two sticks crossed in the dressing room, and he drove equipment managers to distraction trying to make sure players' sticks would never fall across each other by accident and thereby throw him off his game. Esposito also had to wear an old turtleneck shirt, inside out, for every game. He would not stay in hotel rooms whose number ended in unlucky "13." He would only accept gum from a brand-new pack. He had to say Hail Marys and the Lord's Prayer during the anthem. At one point, he refused to let a teammate have his hair cut because he'd become convinced the strength of the team lay, Samson-like, in the player's increasingly long locks. When fans learned of Esposito's obsessions, they began sending him charms, and the player, terrified that throwing one of them out would lead to a bad turn of luck, took to hanging them in his locker until he could barely pick out his equipment from among the rabbits' feet and four-leaf-clover key chains.

A superstition can never be too absurd. At one point, Ottawa Senators forward Bruce Gardiner became so upset with a continuing scoring slump that he took his stick into the washroom and pretended to flush it down the toilet. That night he dramatically broke out of his slump. For the rest of the season, he flushed his stick before each game.

Goaltenders, the eccentrics of the game, are often famous for their superstitions. The late Jacques Plante used to claim he played better if he was wearing underwear he had knitted himself. Patrick Roy, who may go down in history as the greatest goaltender of all, refuses to step on the lines in the ice as he skates to and from his net. In the dressing room between periods, he will obsessively bounce a puck on the floor until it is time to go out, whereupon he will hide the puck so no one can find it.

The early Oilers, however, were Hall-of-Fame believers, and were led, as in all other ways, by Gretzky himself. He always tucked the right side of his jersey into his hockey pants. He had to dress the same way, every practice and every game, always from one side to the other – right, left, right, left – first shin pads, then stockings, skates, elbow pads, gloves. He insisted the equipment manager carry a tin of baby powder which, after he had taped his sticks, he would sprinkle over the tape to "soften" the passes. In pre-game warmups, he would take the first puck, shoot, and deliberately miss the net to the right. After warming up, he would hurry back to the dressing room, where he would drink a Diet Coke, a glass of ice water, a Gatorade, another Diet Coke – and then he would be ready to play.

But before the Oilers would head out onto the ice, they had to go through another series of rituals: booing the start-ing lineup of the other team as each name was read off by Sather; touching one another's gloves; slamming certain players' shin pads; going out in exactly the same order each time. One playoff game, as Paul Coffey was passing by the steel doors that led to the video room, he slammed the butt end of his stick into them. The Oilers won, and a new ritual had been set. In playoffs now, each player in turn rams the butt end of his stick so hard into the doors that it is badly dented, and an Oilers sticker marks each playoff win. Though the Northlands Coliseum has been renamed and remodelled several times over the years since this tradition got started, the battered steel doors remain, an integral part of the team chemistry.

Even the Oilers' equipment staff got involved in those early years. The equipment handlers, Barrie Stafford and Lyle "Sparky" Kulchisky, used to have Trent Evans, by now a building attendant, fill up a bottle – it had to be an empty Snapple iced tea – with snow scraped off the Edmonton ice surface by the Zamboni crew. The melted "Coliseum ice" would then be taken on the road by the Oilers during the spring playoffs and, before each road game, Barrie and Sparky would open the bottle and sprinkle a little Edmonton holy water over the enemy ice surface.

After five Stanley Cups, you don't argue with ritual.

"I've been with a lot of fun teams in my career," says Wayne Gretzky, "but there's something so absolutely special about being an Oiler. It's just *so* unique – everybody feels a part of it. They can argue about where the birthplace of hockey is all they want, but if they want to find out where hockey went to *live*, they'd have to go to Edmonton."

It was while working on the Coliseum ice that Trent Evans first became aware of the strong psychological connection players had to their small rituals and superstitions. The Oilers were playing the Winnipeg Jets in an early playoff series, and one evening Trent happened to be standing at the Zamboni doors as the Jets' starting lineup did a quick skate around their end before the start of the playoff game. Winnipeg's star defenceman Randy Carlyle skated twice around the left circle then immediately over to the corner boards, where he used the black tape on the bottom of his stick to make a small line on the red marking on the boards that indicated where the icing line ran. Once he was satisfied that his special mark was exactly where it had to be, he skated to the Winnipeg goaltender, stuck his stick blade into the top of the net, tapped the goalie twice, and only then was he ready for the opening faceoff. Trent knew a superstition when he saw one, and Carlyle had it really bad.

Before the next game, Trent finished off his ice preparation by rubbing Vaseline in the exact spot where Carlyle left his mark. When the defenceman came out onto the ice, he did his circles, skated to the boards, tried to make his mark but could not. He glowered toward the Zamboni chute as the referee's whistle blew to call the players to the faceoff, but the damage had been done. Carlyle was off his game.

At the next Edmonton game, Trent tried the same thing, only to watch as Carlyle did his two circles, skated to the boards, and then pulled a paper towel out of one of his gloves. He carefully wiped the Vaseline off, made his mark, and, with a big smile toward the Zamboni chute, skated to the goaltender to continue his required ritual.

If little things could come to mean so much, Trent reasoned, then perhaps a loonie at centre ice could serve as inspiration for the Edmonton players who would be coming for the Olympic tournament.

He put the loonie in his pocket, within easy reach for the following morning.

5

THE ICE CREW arrived back at the E Center early the next day. Two workers had been assigned to flood through the night, once every hour, and it had gone well.

Trent, Duncan, and Mike Craig would be in charge of the final floodings, and Trent took the opportunity to head out to centre ice with a screwdriver, where he chipped through the ice until he could see the Canadian dime. He then, very carefully, placed the loonie on top. Using water and the ice slush, he covered up the two coins, and then they continued the flooding throughout the day until there was five-eighths of an inch of ice over the face of the loonie.

When no one else was looking, Trent sneaked back to centre with his camera and took several shots of the coin through the ice. He wondered if anyone walking or driving a Zamboni over his loonie would notice. How closely would they have to look to discover his secret? Even down on his knees with his little flash camera, Trent could be certain it was a loonie only because he had put it there himself.

The ice was too cloudy to make anything out clearly.

He couldn't tell, even kneeling right over it, whether the Queen or the loon was up.

No one would ever notice.

So long as he said nothing, his little secret would be safe.

●

That evening, Trent and Duncan sat up late in their motel room talking about the loonie.

"Just imagine," Duncan said at one point, "what that loonie would be worth if Canada happens to win both gold medals with it down there."

The thought did flash momentarily through Trent Evans' mind. A sports nut, he knew the story about Todd McFarlane, the Calgary comic-book publisher who paid just over three million *American* dollars four years earlier for the baseball St. Louis Cardinals slugger Mark McGwire had hit out of the park for his seventieth home run of the 1998 season. He was well aware that sports memorabilia was one of the main movers on the Internet auction site eBay, with fans around the world bidding for everything from signed hockey skates to – in one unbelievable case – a wad of gum that had been chewed and then spat out by a star ball player.

The loonie would be a natural. If Canada won double gold, it could be like winning the lottery for Trent.

But the more he mulled it over, the more the thought, enticing as it was, didn't sit right.

He could remember one year when Wayne Gretzky's

Oilers had won the Stanley Cup. During the celebratory parade, he had seen a man selling what he called "Northlands Ice" in tiny sealed thimblelike containers he'd attached to small wooden pedestals.

"Here's a guy who's just in it to make a buck," he had thought at the time. "That's got nothing to do with what happened here. That's not what this is all about. I hope people don't buy them."

He couldn't turn around now and become that guy, could he?

At best, he figured, he would have a wonderful memento for his boys. He had already phoned home and told Laurel about the loonie and asked her to tell them in the morning, when they got up. He could imagine them taking it to school for show-and-tell. He could see them hanging on to it for years, as a reminder of the year their father was in the Olympics.

Whatever value the coin had beyond one hundred cents Canadian, Trent figured, would be in its ability to inspire. Loyal to the Oilers, he placed a call to Phoenix, Arizona, where the Oilers were playing one of their final games before the NHL's two-week Olympic break, and he spoke to Sparky Kulchisky, the team's equipment manager and a longtime friend of Gretzky's.

He figured Sparky was the perfect way to get word out to the Oilers coming to Salt Lake City. Manager Kevin Lowe or the equipment handlers could talk it up with the players, and perhaps the loonie would help them get their heads into the Olympics.

Sparky's reaction was so good, so pleasing, that Trent began thinking it couldn't hurt to spread the story a little further. It was one of those secrets that just cried out to be shared, with everyone who heard it delighted to be brought into the loop and promising to keep it quiet, no matter what. Duncan and Mike knew, of course; they had already told a few other Canadians around the rink; and now Trent had told Sparky, who was about to tell a few others.

A CBC crew doing behind-the-scenes features on the Winter Games was filming the ice makers as they put in the E Center ice, and even followed them as Trent and the others were taken up into the mountains to the exclusive lodge where the NHL board of governors were staying. The ice makers had been asked to paint the NHL logo on the little rink outside the lodge, and while they were finishing up, Trent let the loonie story slip to CBC producer Peter Jordan, who got very excited but promised not to leak it, at least until the gold medal game.

Trent drove back wondering what had possessed him to trust the media. Perhaps the altitude had gotten to him. He would have to be more careful with his mouth in the coming days.

The following morning, however, while taking the shuttle to the E Center, he found himself mentioning the loonie to Nate Anderson, the young man who had written to Trent asking him to come to Salt Lake City to make the ice.

The secret, he was about to discover, was already spinning out of control.

"I told too many people."

6

"TAKE IT out."

Trent Evans could hardly believe his ears. The voice belonged to Dan Craig, one of his *mentors* when he'd been learning the craft of ice making at the old Coliseum. But now here he was telling him to get the loonie out of the ice and mark the spot with yellow paint, as he'd been told to do in the first place.

Dan Craig had no choice. He was the NHL representative in charge of the ice, and there had been a complaint from the organizing committee that the Canadians had done something untoward at centre ice. If the Americans had hidden a miniature Stars 'n' Stripes there, Dan Craig knew the Canadians – or the Swedes, Czechs, Russians, Finns, or anyone else in the tournament, for that matter – would be perfectly justified in demanding it be removed.

"Take it out," he repeated.

Dan Craig did not, however, stay around to watch. He delivered his unhappy message to his younger friend and immediately turned and left the building.

Trent found some yellow paint. With Duncan Murie and Mike Craig, he went out to centre ice, miserable that the loonie's moment of glory was over before it had begun. He used a drill to get down to it, and then chipped away at the ice until the loonie was there for the grabbing.

He kneeled back to catch his breath, and then looked around.

The Canadians were all alone.

There were other workers at the Zamboni chute, Americans, but none of them was making sure Trent was following through on Dan Craig's orders. Nor was Dan around to double check.

It was almost as if he had been invited to *pretend* the loonie was being removed.

So Trent Evans did just that. He *pretended* to pick up and pocket the loonie. He placed just enough ice back on it to give a thin film of cover and then he grabbed the paint tin, swirled the yellow paint, and very carefully applied the ordered splotch of paint directly over the loonie.

He then scraped ice back into the hole, smoothed it out, and stood up to admire his work.

Anyone looking down would see a yellow splotch of paint – just as ordered up by Dan Craig, just as they would find in the other three rinks to mark centre ice.

Only here, at the E Center, the splotch of paint would also be serving another purpose: hiding Trent Evans' big secret.

A secret he was now determined to do a better job of keeping.

On Friday, February 8, the Canadian hockey contingent began arriving. On Saturday, Trent saw Wayne Gretzky, Kevin Lowe, and Steve Tambellini checking out the Team Canada dressing room at the E Center and found an opportunity to tell them. They, after all, *had* to know. If the loonie was to be used for inspiration, they would be the ones to decide when, and how.

"I'll give you the loonie if I can get it out after the big game," Trent told Wayne.

Gretzky laughed: "We'll be tripping over each other trying to get at it."

Trent also ran into Bob Nicholson that morning. Nicholson, president of the Canadian Hockey Association, had been the one who talked Gretzky into taking on the job of putting Team Canada together and was the head of the Canadian hockey delegation. He *had* to know as well.

Nicholson's reaction was one of disbelief, but once Trent had convinced him it was no joke, he laughed and embraced the idea completely. In fact, that evening, at a gathering at Canada House in downtown Salt Lake City, Nicholson asked Trent to tell his story to a large group of the hockey crowd, including Pat Quinn and one of the trainers. Trent was nervous, but he got through it okay. Still, he was terrified he was again talking too much about the loonie. If it got out that the coin was still there after he'd been told to get it out, Trent knew he would be in big trouble. He'd likely be ordered home for the remainder of the Olympics.

But the secret held. The hockey was under way, and no one was thinking about anything other than how the teams were doing in the early rounds and how they'd shake down for the critical final round still more than a week away.

There was reason to be apprehensive about both Canadian teams. The women, who had surprised everyone by losing the gold medal to the Americans in Nagano, were now coming off a run of eight consecutive losses to the U.S.A. And there had been concern and debate about the men's team virtually since Gretzky had taken over the job of executive director in November 2000, selected Quinn as his head coach, Ken Hitchcock, Jacques Martin, and the CHA's Wayne Fleming as assistants, and set out to name the team.

The first eight players had to be named by March 23, 2001. Lemieux, in the midst of a remarkable comeback that would see him score thirty-five goals and seventy-six points in only forty-three games, was an obvious choice and had immediately been named captain. But this season he had struggled once again with injury, and was headed to Salt Lake City with a questionable hip and poor, for him, scoring statistics.

More significant, however, had been the story of one player *not* named in the original eight, goaltender Patrick Roy. Roy had been the Canadian netminder in Nagano and had played brilliantly. He was widely believed to be the best Canadian goaltender of the moment, if not of all time, but in the fall, after attending the Team Canada orientation camp in Calgary, he had stunned the country by announcing he would not be going to the Olympics. That left three goaltenders – Curtis Joseph, Martin Brodeur, and Ed Belfour – who seemed to come with almost as many fans doubting their abilities as there were fans cheering for them. Steve Yzerman, another critical player, was hurting even more than Lemieux, with a bad knee that would likely need surgery in the off-season.

Gretzky was philosophical about all the debate over players selected and not selected. It showed, he believed, how much the game mattered to Canadians. What other country, after all, would call a full-blown press conference to announce who would be the third goaltender (Belfour), a player not likely even to see action in the tournament?

The women were also arriving under some controversy. Coach Danielle Sauvageau had cut longtime player Nancy Drolet in mid-January and replaced the veteran with a twenty-year-old rookie, Cherie Piper. There had been great concern about the all-important chemistry of the women's team, and Drolet had even appealed her cut to the CHA, only to be rejected by a three-member panel that heard her case. Sauvageau's reasoning was simple: Drolet had not been pro-ducing, and the Canadian women's team was going to need scoring if it was going to avenge 1998's loss to the Americans.

The women played first, on Day 3 of the sixteen-day Olympic hockey tournament, and they easily defeated Kazakhstan 7-0, with Hayley Wickenheiser, as usual, leading the way with two goals. Even more noteworthy, however, was the play of

Cherie Piper, who scored once and set up another Canadian goal. The Drolet debate was over.

On Day 4, the men's executive held a press conference in which Kevin Lowe announced that, in their minds, the Czechs were "the team to beat" for the gold medal. No one argued the point. The Czech Republic had won the gold medal in Nagano and been the team that dashed Canada's hopes in that infamous shootout that had seen Canada's best player, Wayne Gretzky, left sitting on the bench while, one after another, five Canadian shooters failed to beat Dominik Hasek. The Czechs had also won the last three World Championships, and Hasek, rather than retire as he had threatened, was back at the peak of his game, now playing for the Detroit Red Wings.

On Day 5, the same day the women beat their Russian opponents 7-0, men's coach Pat Quinn and captain Mario Lemieux met with the press. Quinn refused even to speculate on having to face another shootout against the Czech Republic this time.

"My first aim is not even to get there," Quinn told the reporters. "I want to win it straight up, sixty-minute regulation time. Sunday afternoon. I've already seen it."

Of greater concern to the coach was how quickly the Canadian players could come together as a solid team rather than twenty-three gifted individuals. They would play three times in the opening round to decide seeding in the final round, and each of the three final-round games would be like the seventh game of a Stanley Cup series, with victory a must if the team hoped to reach the gold medal final.

"Obviously," said Quinn, "we have to take some shortcuts in team building, but there are some pretty great players coming here. We have five days and three games to shortcut the team-building concept. Those three games we don't have to win, but we intend to win them. Then we have three games we have to win. The progress in those first three games is huge."

Lemieux said he was looking forward to getting going. The expectations were enormous, he admitted, but he welcomed the challenge.

Pressure, claimed the captain, "seems to bring the best out of me. It's something that I enjoy. I don't shy away from it."

7

MARIO LEMIEUX had no idea how quickly that pressure would build. On Day 7, a Friday afternoon, the Canadians were to play their first game. It would be against Sweden, one of the early tournament favourites. The darlings of the Olympic Games, Canadian pairs skaters Jamie Salé and David Pelletier, were even along to watch and, they hoped, bring a little inspiration.

But the Swedes seemed the only ones inspired. On their way to an easy 5-2 victory, they overwhelmed the Canadians and caught them flatfooted with long breakaway passes that took advantage of the absent red line in international hockey.

As Paul Kariya put it right after the final whistle: "It was embarrassing."

"A stinker," said Gretzky.

"We were full of holes," added a red-faced Quinn. "Swiss cheese.

"We have to take this as a lesson. We got hammered. If we don't take that lesson, we'll be going home early."

While the Canadians were reeling from such a lopsided loss in the opening game, no one for a moment thought the loonie at centre ice had somehow hexed them rather than bring its intended good luck.

What had happened *on* the ice was of far greater concern than what was *underneath* it. Curtis Joseph, who had given up the five goals against Sweden, including two to his Toronto Maple Leafs teammate Mats Sundin, would sit out the next game, against Germany. He was replaced by Martin Brodeur, whose father, Denis, had played goal for the Canadian team in the 1956 Winter Games. Mike Peca, who had struggled on the wing, would be moved back to centre. Joe Sakic would be shifted off Lemieux's line in the hopes of spreading the scoring talent around. Lemieux himself might not even be playing, so badly was he in pain from his hip.

The Canadians were also considering going back to the game they knew best, the North American style of short passes, strong defence, and more dump-and-chase than the puck-controlling Swedes had used. There was not enough time to experiment.

●

Trent Evans, in the meantime, was letting the women's team know about the hidden loonie. At one of the practice rinks, he ran into the CHA's Andre Brin, who was handling media for the women, and let Brin in on the secret.

"I love it!" said Brin.

It might serve as a good motivational tool at some point, Trent told him. All he asked was that the story not leave the women's dressing room.

Brin promised. He wasn't telling anyone. He did not even think it was necessary to tell the players. The Canadian women were on the verge of whipping Sweden 11-0, meaning that in only three games the Canadians had outscored their opposition 25-0.

They had no need – *yet* – of a good-luck charm.

It was beginning to seem as if the men's team might not gel quickly enough. On Day 9, they played at The Peaks, this time without an ailing Lemieux, and were barely able to defeat the unheralded German team 3-2, all but blowing a 3-0 lead and fortunate to hang on for the victory against a clearly inferior opponent.

Many believed, in fact, that the Germans could have turned in the upset of the tournament if only Hans Zach, the German coach, had the common sense to pull his goaltender in the dying minutes of the game, when the spunky Germans clearly had the Canadian men on the run.

"A point against Canada would not have helped us in the standings," Zach told a stunned press conference after the match. "And an empty-net goal would have been bad for our self-confidence."

The Canadians were trying to show a stiff upper lip. Paul Kariya said the win was important, not the showing, and that soon enough the players would be in sync with one another.

The next day, Day 10, a bit of that missing chemistry was found. At the E Center, with the coin at centre ice, the men played their 1998 nemesis, the Czech Republic, with Dominik Hasek in net. They came out of the game with an impressive 3-3 tie that featured an uncanny third-period save by Martin Brodeur. Brodeur had appeared cleanly beaten on a cross-ice pass, only to lunge back into the net in desperation, knocking the puck away just as Czech forward Jan Hrdina sent it flying into the open side. Gretzky would later claim that Brodeur's save was the "turning point in the Olympics for us."

The game also marked the successful return of Mario Lemieux. He scored twice against Hasek, the first time slipping an effortless shot through Hasek's five-hole, the second on a disputed goal that had to go to video review, where it was determined that Lemieux's shot had been stopped by Hasek's glove but that the glove had crossed over the goal line, just as Lemieux had claimed.

Brodeur's magnificent save had fired up the Canadians, and instead of being down 4-2, they were able to come back and tie the match after Joe Nieuwendyk knocked a Theoren Fleury pass out of the air and in behind Hasek. The goal had been followed, instantly, by a vicious cross-check to Fleury's back by Czech defenceman Roman Hamrlik, a play that very nearly led to an on-ice brawl between the two longtime rivals.

"We didn't win," Brodeur told reporters on his way off the ice, "but in our hearts, the way we played, we felt like we won."

The Czechs, however, were quick to dismiss the tie – and their opponent.

"We don't care about Canada," said forward Martin Rucinsky. "We don't take them as the team to beat. I don't think they're even close to being the best team in the tournament. You've seen that by the scores."

Czech captain Jaromir Jagr, however, wasn't sure there was anything to conclude from what he had seen so far, either on the ice or on the scoreboard.

"The best team doesn't win this tournament," Jagr said as he left the ice.

"The luckiest team does."

8

WAYNE GRETZKY had been growing increasingly intense. The cameras had found him in the stands, game in, game out, with his face buried in his hands, or wearing the same stunned and dejected look Canadians had seen four years earlier when he sat, alone, on the Canadian bench in Nagano, long after the ill-fated shootout had decided in favour of the Czechs.

But if he had felt helpless in Nagano as other players were selected to take the five shots for Canada, it was nothing to how he felt in Salt Lake City.

"There's no question," he said, "it's harder to watch a game than it is to play. It's a much more stressful situation to watch. When you play and make a mistake, you can go out there on your next shift and do something about it. When you're sitting on top, it's much more difficult."

Just before Team Canada's game against the Czech Republic in the opening round, the cameras found Gretzky sitting in a brand-new seat: the players' bench. But not dressed to play, not making a surprise comeback; he was sitting on the bench in his Team Canada blazer, watching the warmup with Kevin Lowe.

"We tried to change our luck," Gretzky said, smiling rather sheepishly when asked why he had gone down there to sit.

"I just felt we had to show the players that they weren't the only ones really into this, that all the coaches and managers and support staff were – the whole country was."

So they sat on the bench during the warmup, and Team Canada, finally, had played up to its potential.

Every warmup from now on, they would sit on the bench. It had worked once; it would work again.

Gretzky wasn't alone in developing a new habit. Bob Nicholson had turned up for Canada's first win, against Germany, wearing a red turtleneck instead of his usual tie. Not only that, but Steve Tambellini happened to notice it was on inside out and backwards, a good sign as to how nervous the president of the Canadian Hockey Association had become following the team's 5-2 loss to Sweden. After the win, Nicholson decided from then on he would wear a tie for the women's games only; the turtleneck would be reserved for the men's. Tambellini took it one step further, insisting that Nicholson's red turtleneck be worn inside out and backwards, no matter how embarrassed Nicholson might become.

"It was getting nuts," says Nicholson. "I saw Steve that day, and he says, '*Got it on? Got it on inside out?*' and I said I did, and he seemed satisfied with that."

Even Trent Evans was getting into the act. Each day, under his volunteer uniform, he was wearing his lucky T-shirt – a

Molson Canadian T-shirt with "Go Canada Go!" across the front.

The morning before the tie against the Czechs, Gretzky, Lowe, and Tambellini had gone with Wayne's father, Walter, and Gretzky family friend Charlie Henry to Denny's for breakfast, as they had most mornings since they arrived in Salt Lake City. This time, however, Hall-of-Famer Lanny McDonald was there too.

They had arrived exactly at eight, the time they had agreed to meet McDonald. Gretzky ordered pancakes and bacon.

From now on, every morning at eight they would meet at Denny's restaurant and McDonald would join them. And every morning for the rest of the Olympics, Wayne Gretzky would order exactly the same breakfast: pancakes and bacon.

"It was crazy," says Gretzky. "Word got around that we were eating breakfast there every morning, and soon it seemed like every Canadian fan in Salt Lake City was having breakfast at the same Denny's. We had to make special arrangements to have a booth, because by the end, when we'd get there at eight, there would already be a long line of Canadians stretching right out the door waiting for tables. We were barely able to get the seat we wanted some mornings."

Routine mattered terribly to Gretzky. It had mattered to him since he was a child just learning the game, and he picked up certain habits then that would stick with him all his life. The sweater tucked in on one side, for example, had been an idea of Walter's. He took one look at his tiny boy in the over-sized sweater of his first team and decided he'd better tuck it in on the shooting side, or else the boy's arm might get caught in his own sweater. Thirty years later, an NHL veteran and six feet tall, Wayne was still tucking in the sweater.

"It's not all superstition," he says. "It's more about routine, a routine that you don't want to break."

Once the game against the Czechs was over, however, Gretzky did something so beyond his usual routine that he stunned the press gathered to hear the post-game comments. Renowned for his diplomacy, Gretzky suddenly turned angry. He went into a long rant about Hamrlik's cross-check, the overall officiating of the Olympics, and the attitude of the rest of the world toward Canada. No one at the gathering had ever seen Gretzky like this before.

When asked whether Canada's slow start could be tied to a "lack of respect" for the international game, Gretzky snapped.

"No, no, not at all," a visibly angry Gretzky answered. "To a man, everyone in there will tell you how great a player Hasek is, they'll tell you how great Sundin is. They'll tell you how good Jagr is. So we know they're good players.

"I don't think we dislike those countries as much as they hate us. And that's a fact. They don't like us. They want to see us fail. They love beating us. They might tell you guys something different, but believe me, when you're on the ice, that's what they say. They don't like us, and we've got to get that same feeling towards them.

"I mean, right now, it's comical listening to the things that are being said. It almost sickens my stomach to turn the TV on, because I'm such a proud Canadian and such a fan of our game and very proud of all the players in our locker-room, and it makes me ill to hear some of the things that are being said about us."

He didn't stop there. In answer to further questions, he talked about how Canadian players have always been accused of "hooliganism." If a Canadian had done to a Czech what Hamrlik had done to Fleury, he said, it would be an international incident.

"They talk about how we're not a skating team," Gretzky continued, still steamed, "we can't move the puck, we have no finesse. That's crazy. We skated them into the ground in the third period. There should've been four or five penalties, blatant penalties, and there should've been two or three suspensions.

"Am I hot? Yeah, I'm hot, because I'm tired of people taking shots at Canadian hockey. When we do it, we're hooligans. When Europeans do it, it's okay, because they're not tough or they're not dirty.

"Well, that's a crock of crap."

Gretzky then turned his rising anger on the host Americans. Rumours about players on Team Canada being upset with Quinn's coaching style, he said, were nothing but "American propaganda." He excused the U.S. Olympic team – with several of his closest friends on the roster – but not the U.S. media or the Salt Lake City organizers.

"If you want to talk about hockey," he said, "you want to talk about the Canadians, because we're the biggest story down here in hockey. And they're loving us not doing well. They loved the start we had. It's a big story for them. . . .

"People don't understand the pressure these guys are under. They don't understand the BS that our guys have to go through. And we're still here, we're still standing, and we're very proud. We're proud players . . .

"Believe me, we've got a proud bunch in our locker room. I know the whole world wants us to lose, except for Canada and Canada's fans and our players, and we'll be there.

"We'll be standing."

It was an extraordinary and unexpected performance. Someone asked Walter Gretzky if he'd ever seen his son like this before, and Walter shook his head and said, "Privately, yes. Not publicly, though."

9

THE WOMEN played the following day and finally allowed a goal. Three, in fact. The feisty little Finns made a game of it for a while, erasing a 2-0 Canada lead by scoring three times and holding on to the lead for nearly a full period's worth of hockey. Hayley Wickenheiser tied the game barely three minutes into the third period, however, and six seconds later – a women's Olympic record – Jayna Hefford put Canada ahead to stay.

But the big story was still Wayne Gretzky's comments following the 3-3 tie against the Czech Republic. He claimed he had no regrets about what he'd said, but that night he had hardly slept at all.

Privately, he wondered if maybe he'd gone too far.

The morning after his outburst, he had met the same crowd as usual at eight o'clock at Denny's. Over pancakes and bacon, he asked Kevin Lowe and Steve Tambellini what they thought about the performance.

"You really let the bees out of the beehive, didn't you?" Lowe said.

Gretzky looked up from his plate, worried.

"Do you think I went too far?"

"No, no," said Tambellini. "This might be just the thing to rally the troops."

Perhaps it was. The rant was given several different twists in the media. Was Gretzky cracking under the pressure? Was he simply doing what Glen Sather used to do by being purposely controversial to draw attention off the players? Was it a move calculated to light a fire under the team? But in the end, the reason for it mattered far less than the result. Team Canada had found its focus. It had chemistry. It had, as Pat Quinn said it must, taken a shortcut and become a real *team*.

From this point on, each game would count for everything. On the women's side, the Canadians and Americans were marching irrevocably toward another gold medal showdown. But it was not so clear cut on the men's side. The Swedes had overtaken the Czechs as the tournament favourites, and the Americans were looking far stronger than anyone had anticipated. Perhaps it was the home-ice advantage, perhaps the surge of patriotism that had followed the tragedies the previous September – whatever it was, the Americans were a force. The Czechs were still strong, had tied the Canadians after all, and the Russians seemed on the verge of finding their feet as well. Any one of six men's teams could claim gold – but only two of them would have a chance to play for it.

But then, early in the afternoon of Day 12, there was a change of luck so spectacular no one could quite believe it. Many still have trouble believing what happened. Little Belarus beat mighty Sweden at the E Center, 4-3, on a shot from centre ice by defenceman Vladimir Kopat with 2:24 left in the game. Kopat would have missed the Swedish net had netminder Tommy Salo not let the puck glance off his glove, then his mask, then roll down his back and over the goal line as slowly as a curling stone sliding onto the button of the house.

As grinning Belarus goaltender Andrei Mezin put it after the match: "Sometimes even a gun without bullets shoots."

The Swedes, supposedly on their way to the final when the puck dropped at the start of the game, were on their way home when the buzzer sounded just over two hours later.

●

Team Canada was well prepared for its game against the Finns. Gretzky had had his pancakes and bacon for breakfast. Lanny McDonald had joined them in their usual Denny's booth. Nicholson had his red turtleneck on, inside out and backwards, as confirmed by Tambellini. Gretzky and Lowe were sitting on the players' bench during the warmup. Trent Evans had his Molson T-shirt on underneath his green volunteer's uniform.

And the loonie was still in the ice.

Trent knew this for certain. With the arena emptied between matches, he had slipped out to centre ice with his battery-driven drill and quickly drilled down until he struck metal. Not cement, but metal. The loonie was still there.

It would be the first of three or so mysterious "dents" that would be visible on the loonie when they took it to the Hockey Hall of Fame.

Strange things were happening in the tournament. Belarus had finished off Sweden, and now the Czechs, the defending Olympic champions, were gone as well, eliminated 1-0 by the suddenly awakened Russians. The Americans, on the other hand, were getting stronger each game, having just routed Germany 5-0.

Traditionally, however, the Canadians always had trouble against the Finns, perhaps because the Finnish style of play was so similar to the Canadian – tough, fearless hockey – and they had skilled players to match the best of the Canadians.

They did not, however, have Mario Lemieux, and late in the second period Lemieux broke in with Steve Yzerman, seemed in a good position to shoot, but delayed perfectly and slipped a lovely pass to Yzerman, who had an empty net to welcome the winning goal. Even the goal scorer had been fooled by the play. "I thought *he* was going to shoot," said a laughing Yzerman after Team Canada's 2-1 victory.

Canadian confidence was climbing, the pressure eased, the anxiety back home suddenly lifting. "I guess all the pharmacies in Canada will have to close now," joked Theo Fleury.

The reason was obvious. Having gotten by Finland, Canada now had only to beat Belarus in the semi-final game to play for the gold medal. The path ahead suddenly seemed clear for the first time.

One person, however, was still extremely concerned. It was the executive director of Team Canada, Wayne Gretzky.

"Honest to God," he remembers, "for the next five days after I'd spoken out, I was just beside myself with worry. I couldn't sleep. I couldn't stop wondering if I really had gone too far. Had I instead fired up the other teams? I was terrified of the game against Finland, because they always played Canada so well, and they have so much heart on that team. And we barely squeaked through 2-1.

"But that was just about the time when we started to get some real luck. Sweden lost to Belarus on that fluke goal. That should never have happened, but in the Olympics, with just one game, anything can happen, and in this case it did happen.

"I was still convinced we needed a blowout, one game where everything would come together and work for us. Sweden had one right off the start – against us! – and the Americans had one against Belarus.

"We should have had ours against Germany, but instead it almost backfired on us. We'd gone up 3-0 and it should have ended 6-0 or even higher. But what happened? It ends 3-2 and we're hanging on by our teeth for that win.

"That game was at The Peaks, and as we were driving back – it took about an hour and a half – I was in pretty bad shape. I just kept thinking, 'Oh, my goodness, what's going on here? What's happening? What's wrong with us? We have a good team, we have a *great* team – but it's not working.'

"Looking back now, I think the point where our luck turned was when Marty made that great save for us against the Czechs. Right then, I figured, we can hardly wait to get the Swedes again and show them just how we can play this game. It was going to be completely different, I was convinced of that.

"But then we got really lucky. Belarus beats Sweden, the Czechs are put out, and we get to play Belarus to reach the gold medal game. And all of a sudden, we're seen as the team to beat.

"We'd had such bad luck in Nagano, losing that shootout against the Czechs, and in 1994 we'd lost another shootout against the Swedes for the gold medal.

"Maybe it was our time to get a little luck."

10

THE NEXT day the men's team held an optional practice, and Gretzky insisted on going out to the rink to see for himself what the mood was like. He could hardly believe his eyes when he walked in. There were players all over the ice, but one player in particular caught his eye.

Number 66, Mario Lemieux.

Gretzky called over one of the trainers. "What's Mario doing out there?" he demanded. "He's hurt."

"He says his hip's fine," answered the trainer.

"It's not his hip," laughed Gretzky. "He's got amnesia! Did he forget this was an optional?"

That evening, the men's team went to the E Center to watch the women's gold medal game. It was the match that had been predicted for the previous four years: U.S.A. versus Canada, the same two teams that had met in Nagano.

Canada had been expected to win in Nagano; now the Americans were the clear favourites. They were playing on home ice before a pumped crowd. They had breezed through their games to get here, looking stronger every period. And they had beaten the Canadian women eight times in a row heading into the 2002 Winter Games.

Trent Evans was worried enough about the outcome that he took a chance in the run-up to the late-afternoon match at the E Center. He was doing a flood when he noticed several of the Canadian women coming out onto the bench to tape their sticks and simply soak up the atmosphere before the warmup got under way. Hayley Wickenheiser was there, and Danielle Goyette, and two or three others.

Trent walked over, introduced himself, said he was from Edmonton and that he'd be doing the ice for their game. Then he told them about the loonie at centre ice, how it was there to bring them good luck.

In fact, many of them already knew about it.

"We heard about it earlier that day, while we were on the bus going from the athletes' village to the E Center," remembers Cassie Campbell, captain of the women's team. "It was like a rumour that just raced through the bus. There was nothing formal, no big announcement, but someone – it must have been Wayne Gretzky – had told our coaching staff, and now we knew about it and we knew it was to be kept a secret. I thought the idea was really cool, really neat."

"I heard about it from Cassie before the game," Jayna Hefford recalls, "but Hayley also spoke about it to the team between the first and second period.

"It was pretty neat. It was also kind of a surprise to think that something like that could happen in the United States. It gave us a little extra pride. It's strange when you get to the Olympics, but every time you hear the word 'Canada' or see

'Canada,' it does something to you, and this was just one more little thing that made us think about who we were and what we were trying to do."

The Canadian women would need every edge they could get. They scored first, fortunately, early in the game, when Caroline Ouellette was set up by Cherie Piper, the late addition to the team. But the Americans pressed back with determination, and Canadian goaltender Kim St. Pierre had to be sharp in the second half of the opening period when Canada was given four penalties in a row.

By the middle of the second period, it had been *eight* penalties in a row. The referee appeared to be giving the home team every imaginable opportunity, and though Team U.S.A. did tie the game briefly, Canada went ahead again on a goal by Hayley Wickenheiser. And then, with only one second left in the second period, Jayna Hefford picked up her own rebound and scored what would prove to be the gold-medal-winning goal. Canada won 3-2.

The horn went, and the Canadian women poured over the boards, throwing sticks and gloves and helmets into the air as they jumped into each other's arms and right on top of Kim St. Pierre.

The Zamboni doors opened and Trent Evans was among the crew sent out to push the discarded equipment against the boards so that none of the dignitaries coming out for the medal ceremony would trip. He was piling gloves and sticks up against the Team Canada bench when he saw something that almost stopped his heart.

The Canadian women were lining up at their blueline for the post-game ceremonies, but three of the players had skated ahead to centre ice.

One of them, Therese Brisson, was down on one knee and *pointing at the loonie!* The other two, Danielle Goyette and Geraldine Heaney, were staring down at where Brisson was pointing.

"I panicked," remembers Trent, "absolutely panicked. I ran and found Bob Nicholson, and I started shouting at him, *'Get them away from centre! Get them away!'* and he started moving toward them, but Andre Brin was already there shouting at them."

What Trent didn't know was that the scene at centre ice had already been spotted from high up in the stands by someone who panicked even more than he did.

Wayne Gretzky.

"That was the first time I really thought about the loonie after hearing about it from Trent. We had just won the gold medal in women's hockey, despite all the penalties, despite the clear bias of the refereeing, and I was sitting there thinking that now it was destiny – that we were going to win not one gold, but two. It was fate.

"Then I saw the women at centre, and I had no way of getting down there, but I saw Brad Pascall was on the ice, and so I got on my cellphone and started yelling over the sounds of the crowd.

"*'Get those girls outta there!'* I shouted, *'They're going to ruin it!'*"

A Loonie for Luck

Pascall was surprised he even heard his phone ring over the sound of the crowd. He answered it instinctively. "It was Gretzky, and he was screaming, '*Tell them to get away! We need it for our game!*' and I tried running, but I had leather shoes on, and all I did was slip. So I used my phone to call Andre, who was closer to them. '*Get them away!*' I was yelling. '*Get them away!*'"

Hayley Wickenheiser had noticed as well, and even though she had her son, Noah, in her arms, and had just been told she'd been named MVP for the tournament, she was worrying about the loonie.

"I went and kissed centre ice," said Danielle Goyette. "Hayley came over and said to me, 'Get away, Danielle. We can't tell people it's there. The men's final is in three days, and we have to keep it secret!'"

The women moved off, but others had noticed. Trent Evans was beside himself with worry. He was certain the secret had been blown.

One who had noticed was John Davidson, the former goaltender who was now doing colour commentary at the games for NBC. He had seen the women at centre, and it aroused his curiosity.

Davidson caught up with Gretzky after the match and asked if his friend knew what was up with the women's scene at centre ice.

"What do you mean?" Gretzky asked, trying to look as puzzled as possible.

"It looked like they were *kissing* the ice."

73

"Well," said Gretzky, "they were. That's what Salé and Pelletier did after they skated, remember? Now all the Canadians are doing it."

Davidson nodded. "Oh, yeah. That makes sense."

It did not, of course, but Gretzky was relieved. He figured if John Davidson – probably the best-connected broadcaster in hockey – didn't know about the loonie, then no one outside the small inner circle knew.

Trent Evans wasn't so sure. There was no way, he thought, the secret could hold through Sunday. He knew that the CBC was sitting on the story, but he had no idea how long the Canadian broadcaster would be willing to keep it to themselves. He knew there were dozens upon dozens of people in the Olympic Village who knew about the coin, and surely they would be telling others, who would in turn tell others. There was also the chance that, at any moment, one of the Americans on the ice-making crew or one of the organizers might decide to check centre ice and see if there was indeed anything under that yellow splotch of paint.

And there were some things he was better off *not* knowing.

Long after the women's gold medal game had been settled, after "O Canada" had been played and the gold, silver, and bronze medals handed out, after the ice had been cleared and the stands emptied and everyone else had gone home, some of the women remained in the dressing room, still partying.

"Five of us," remembers Jayna Hefford, "me, Vicky Sunohara, Lori Dupuis, Caroline Ouellette, and Isabelle Chartrand, all went out in our flip-flops to centre ice. We had half our gear on, and we were all carrying beer and drinking it, and we all stood at centre ice and saluted the loonie with our beer and then took pictures of each other standing there.

"There was no one else around. No one saw us there. No one gave away the secret."

11

WAYNE GRETZKY finally got his longed-for "blowout." Little Belarus, having already won its personal "gold medal" in that unexpected upset against Sweden earlier in the week, put up next to no fight against the larger and more-skilled Canadians. They went down 7-1.

"It was important for us to win by a big margin," said Mario Lemieux.

The crowd, heavily dominated by Canadian fans – many of them dressed in 1972 Team Canada replica jerseys – sang "O Canada" as the game wound down and chanted "*Russia! Russia!*" in the hopes of a repeat of the legendary '72 Summit Series, which Canada had won over the old Soviet Union.

Four hours later, however, the opponent was decided with a Team U.S.A. win over the Russians, a 3-2 victory that would be remembered for the way the Russians dominated in the third period and yet could not score the goal required to send the game into overtime. On one power play alone, the Russians hit the post twice and argued, unsuccessfully, that one of their shots had actually gone in. The officials refused to go to video replay. The game ended on an ugly note, with the Russians all but attacking referee Bill McCreary.

The gold medal would be decided between the home favourites and the Canadians. American forward Jeremy Roenick, who had played his junior hockey in Hull, Quebec, put the upcoming match in perfect perspective: "I don't think there will be one person on the street anywhere in Canada Sunday afternoon."

The buildup over the next two days was extraordinary. The executive of the men's team was so brimming with high expectations that on Saturday night they sat around talking about who was going to be the next Paul Henderson. Who would score the winning goal? Who would be Canada's hero?

Now it was Trent Evans who could not sleep. He was certain word about the loonie was going to get out. He had even called his family back in Canada to see if a replacement loonie could be couriered to him in time. When that seemed impossible, he asked around and Kevin Lowe came up with one and handed it over, just in case.

Playing the Americans in the gold medal match only increased the likelihood the loonie wouldn't survive. If any of the American ice makers or organizers knew it was still there, it would not remain for long. Trent would be found responsible for not removing it and be in deep, deep trouble.

Saturday night he heard that the CBC had gone with the loonie story that evening during the set-up for Sunday's gold medal match. He called his brother, Darren, a golf professional in Barrie, Ontario, and asked if he'd been watching the CBC. Darren confirmed that they'd just done a piece on the loonie in the ice.

Trent could not believe it. The story had been broadcast across Canada and somehow hadn't made it over the border. No one had seen it. No one had phoned about it. Miraculously, in Salt Lake City, it remained a secret.

By noon on Sunday, Day 16, there was a sea of American and Canadian colours around the E Center. Some Canadians were holding tickets they had purchased for as much as U.S. $2,750 on the Internet. It was predicted that the television audience in Canada was going to be the largest ever to watch a sporting event. National Hockey League rinks were being opened up to allow fans to watch on the scoreboard screens. Big screens were being set up in Vancouver and in Calgary's Olympic Park. Canadian soldiers were gathering with American soldiers in Kandahar, Afghanistan, to watch the game and cheer for their teams.

Jeremy Roenick had predicted there wouldn't be a person in the streets of Canada when the puck was dropped, and it seemed he was right. The entire country had come to a standstill. It was almost as if thirty-one million people had decided to hold their breath at the same time. Only once before, in 1972, had the country's reputation in hockey been so clearly on the line.

Trent had arrived early. The first thing he did was grab his drill and head out to centre ice, where he plunged the drill hard into the ice and, in his mind, struck gold.

The loonie was still there.

And now it had another dent – a large one.

Just in case, he had the replacement loonie in his pocket. If someone was going to pull the loonie out, he was going to do everything he could to get another one back in.

Playing the Americans, on the Americans' home ice, in front of a crowd in a patriotic frenzy, the Canadians would need every break they could get – from wherever they could get it. A lucky coin might turn into a lucky bounce, which could ultimately turn gold.

"I told the players just before the game," remembers Gretzky. "I went into the locker room and told them that the ice makers from Edmonton had hidden a loonie in the ice for good luck."

Gretzky told the players to tap the ice as they skated by it, and several did during the warmup – with Gretzky and Lowe sitting once again on the players' bench, observing – and Mario Lemieux made certain to tap the ice just before the puck dropped to start the game.

Trent, by now a nervous wreck, was watching from the Zamboni chute. Even after the puck did drop and the game began, he could not stop fretting. They could remove the coin between periods if word came down – perhaps even now some American who had seen the CBC telecast was calling. It could be taken out and the ice repaired in less than twenty seconds. They could even do it, he figured, in a stoppage of play.

Roy MacGregor

The Americans scored first when Canada's Owen Nolan made an error clearing the puck in his own end, and Doug Weight and Tony Amonte flew down the ice on a two-on-one break, Amonte firing the puck between Brodeur's pads.

It seemed too easy. An *un*lucky bounce for Nolan had turned into too easy a break, too easy a goal.

Six minutes later, Mario Lemieux made the play of the tournament without even touching the puck. He deliberately let a pass from Chris Pronger slip between his legs to Paul Kariya, waiting on his left, and Kariya scored into a virtually open net behind American goaltender Mike Richter.

"He is sneaky," an admiring Richter would later say of Lemieux. "He has such a good hockey sense. He knows Kariya is there. I can see them both, and the pass goes to Mario's stick. He doesn't just not play it, he actually puts his stick there to play it and then moves his stick. It was a beautiful play – a play you have to honour as a goalie."

The goal brought Canada to life. Less than four minutes later, Jarome Iginla shovelled in a hard Joe Sakic pass that came to him at the side of the crease.

Canada should have gone up by two goals in the second period when, with a two-man advantage, Lemieux – playing brilliantly on a line with Kariya and Yzerman – inexplicably missed an open net when he misfired and put the puck off the goalpost. Shortly after, the Americans tied the game again on a power play when a shot went in off the stick of Canadian defenceman Chris Pronger.

But then Canada got lucky. *Very* lucky.

And just in time.

A Loonie for Luck

With less than two minutes to go in the second period, Sakic merely lofted a wrist shot toward the U.S. net, whereupon it hit a stick and dribbled, somehow, in behind a falling Richter.

The Americans pressed in the third, and seemed to rally just as luck struck again – and again in Canada's favour.

Steve Yzerman, one of the game's cleaner players, had been in the penalty box when he stepped out to meet a puck that happily chanced to be headed his way. Yzerman, who is also one of the game's great passers, sent the puck to Iginla, who fired a heavy shot that bulldozed right through Richter's glove, hit the ice, and rolled over the goal line.

It was at this exact point, 16:01 of the third period, that Wayne Gretzky knew how it would end. He leapt out of his seat and threw his arms in the air.

With that goal, the extraordinary pressure that defenceman Al MacInnis would describe as the equivalent of walking around with "a piano on your back," was magically, and forever, lifted.

Less than three minutes later, Iginla sent Sakic in on a breakaway, and Sakic scored to make it 5-2. With only 1:20 left on the clock, the gold medal game was out of reach for the Americans and, finally, within the grasp of Canada.

Gold – fifty years to the day since the Edmonton Mercurys won gold in Oslo.

Double gold – men and women!

And the loonie had survived.

12

IN THE Canadian men's ceremonial team picture, a man in a green suit can be seen in the background just over the shoulder of Canadian defenceman Al MacInnis. It is Trent Evans. He is standing on the Canadian bench and has two things in his hand, a screwdriver and a bottle of hot water.

As soon as the photograph was taken, Trent hurried over to Kevin Lowe and asked Lowe to stay with him while the two of them went to centre ice. Trent didn't want to run the risk of being told to get off the ice because he wasn't part of the team.

Both men huddled over centre ice while Trent emptied the contents of the water bottle. Then, with the ice melting, Trent chipped away the yellow paint that covered the loonie. He picked it out, handed it to Lowe, who handed it right back.

"No," said Lowe, "you give it to Gretz. You're the guy who put it there."

Gretzky, however, was on the phone, fielding a congratulatory call from the prime minister of Canada, Jean Chrétien.

It was pandemonium on the ice, with equipment everywhere and the players all over one another, back-slapping and hugging and yelling that they'd won the gold medal.

There was no doubt they knew they were part of history: the first gold medal for Canada in men's hockey in fifty years *to the exact day*. Owen Nolan had been so aware of the moment's significance that, with some two minutes still remaining in the game, he had bolted from the bench to the dressing room and raced back with his video camera so he could record the last few moments of his part in sports history.

"What if they'd wanted you on the ice?" a Canadian reporter asked him.

"No way!" he'd shouted, laughing. "I wasn't going – I was *busy!*"

Al MacInnis, the oldest player on the team at thirty-eight, knew that something like this could happen only once in a lifetime. "I told the young guys like Jarome and Simon Gagné to cherish this game, because you never know," MacInnis said as the players left the ice with their gold medals hanging around their necks.

"I'll look back at this medal, whether it's fifteen, twenty, or ten years – as long as I'm alive."

Trent Evans, in the meantime, was marching around the corridors of the E Center with the loonie in his right hand, squeezing it so tight it's a wonder it didn't give change.

"I felt like a kid who'd just robbed a candy store. But I was afraid even to stop and look at it for fear someone would see me. I didn't know if anyone had seen me at centre ice with

Kevin. I didn't know if the organizers even knew about it. All I knew for sure was I'd been told to take it out and I hadn't, so I figured someone was going to be upset about it for sure."

Then he remembered something: *he'd forgotten the dime*.

"I'd been in such a hurry to get the loonie out I'd never even thought about it. I circled the building once more and then went back out onto the ice to get the dime. It was just lying there where Kevin and I had melted away the ice. Anyone could have picked it up."

He scooped it up and hid it away in a pocket separate from his other change. Then he circled the building a couple more times, still clutching the loonie in his right hand. Finally, as he neared the Team Canada dressing room, he saw Andre Brin standing outside the door.

"I've got the loonie," he shouted over the yelling still coming from the room.

"Get in here!" Brin called back, moving people aside so Trent would have a clear path into the room.

The players were celebrating the awarding of the tournament MVP award to Joe Sakic – the fifteenth pick back in 1987 – as Trent entered, and for a moment he wondered if anyone would have time at all for his loonie.

But almost as soon as Trent got inside the dressing room, Gretzky caught his eye and called him over. Trent attempted to hand over the loonie, but Gretzky would have none of it until he had called Mario Lemieux over and they were able to capture the moment on camera.

Trent was so excited, all he could do was stand there and giggle.

Gretzky asked if he could borrow the loonie for a minute, and Trent, having no idea what the executive director of Team Canada was planning to do with it, nodded in agreement. To Trent's amazement – and slight concern – Gretzky slipped the coin in the left pocket of his jacket and left the room.

Moments later, at a press conference, Gretzky reached back into the pocket, took out the loonie, and held it up for the international media to see.

He told the story of the coin being buried at centre ice for the entire tournament to bring the Canadian hockey teams luck – and how it had brought them two gold medals.

"The ice maker was from Canada," Gretzky explained.

The American media had no idea what the coin was.

"Loonie," explained Gretzky, grinning from ear to ear. He spelled it out. "L-o-o-n-i-e. Like the bird. No, it's not real gold. It's worth about sixty-four cents U.S.

"It was for good luck. So I guess it worked.

"I know Canadian people are having a great time from coast to coast. They've waited a long time for this. Our country really desperately needed to win this tournament."

Gretzky even joked about the risk taken by Trent and the other Canadian ice makers. "I don't know if they'll lose their jobs," he told the media scrambling to get the story. "I hope not – but we got two gold medals out of it.

"And the coin will look pretty good, I think, in the Hall of Fame."

With the international media still scratching their heads over what a "loonie" was and what it had meant to the

Canadians, Gretzky returned to the dressing room, where he brushed past Trent Evans and paused to pat his back and whisper in his ear.

"You're going to be a legend," he predicted.

Gretzky then handed the coin to NHL commissioner Gary Bettman, who had come to offer congratulations to the players. Bettman had watched the press conference, knew the story, and was delighted with it.

"This has to be in the Hall of Fame," Gretzky said.

Bettman readily agreed.

Phil Pritchard, the Hall of Fame's guardian of the Stanley Cup, also happened to be in the room and was called over for a press shot of Gretzky handing the coin over for safe keeping.

"Whatever you do," Gretzky said to Pritchard as cameras flashed in front of them, "don't use it in a pop machine."

14

TRENT EVANS was on his way home. He hadn't seen his family in three weeks and had missed them terribly. Just talking to the boys on the phone had brought him to tears. But now, instead of being met by them at the airport, he was fielding calls along the way warning him that so many television crews would be there he might not be able to find his family in the crush.

He had never expected this. The story of the loonie was a sensation on the sports pages around the world.

An article by Bill Plaschke of the *Los Angeles Times* began:

> They were singing in Saskatchewan, howling in Halifax, waltzing in Winnipeg.
>
> Okay, maybe not waltzing in Winnipeg.
>
> But oh, Canada was partying Sunday night, dancing all over its home and native land, true patriot love flowing from the taps in celebration of a group of brave and hearty souls that just busted a 50-year losing streak.

A Loonie for Luck

The men's hockey team?

No, silly, the E Center ice-making crew.

Shortly after Canada defeated the United States, 5-2, in the Winter Olympic gold medal hockey game, team boss Wayne Gretzky admitted that the hero was not Joe Sakic, but a couple of Joe Schmoes . . .

But the story was bigger than the sports pages. CBC's *The National* had called. They were looking for Trent Evans to do a one-on-one interview with news anchor Peter Mansbridge.

And in the Alberta provincial legislature, Premier Ralph Klein was making a speech about the event. "Canada's pride," the premier began, "was not only evident in the performance of the nation's athletes, it was fuelled by a mischievous act of true Canadian spirit. A young gentleman by the name of Mr. Trent Evans, as members of the Assembly have probably heard, is the renowned Edmonton ice maker who was part of the ice crew for the Olympic hockey tournaments. In the course of his work, Mr. Evans quietly planted a Canadian loonie beneath the surface of centre ice.

"Now I don't know if this act brought good luck to the Canadian hockey teams. The fact that both teams won gold suggests that they didn't need any good-luck charms, but the gesture by Mr. Evans was a true indication that the Canadian spirit is difficult, if not impossible, to repress."

One of those cheering Klein from the front benches was the minister of children's services, Iris Evans, Trent's mother.

All the attention was far more than Trent Evans had ever anticipated, or figured he deserved.

"I would never say Team Canada won because the loonie was there," he says. "It was just part of the atmosphere. They won, and if the loonie played some small part in superstition or luck or whatever, then that's just great. That's the best I could have hoped for when I put it there."

But others thought the story was so perfect it was destined from the beginning to become a legend.

"I loved it right from the start," says Bob Nicholson. "For me, the loonie represents all those Canadians who do so much for the game, the volunteers, the organizers, the ice makers, the coaches, managers, trainers, parents – everyone. We're the best country in the world at the game, and we're the best in the world at making the ice that the game is played on. It was one way of showing that everyone in Canada had some small part to play."

"It was just a kind of subtle inspiration," says Cassie Campbell, the women's captain. "In a way it almost makes the story *too* perfect, both Canadian teams winning gold and the loonie being hidden in the ice, but in another way it was, for us, kind of like we were playing in Canada.

"The loonie was perfect. It was a perfect symbol of how important hockey is to Canadians – that some guy from Edmonton would literally put his job on the line to make sure we had a little piece of Canada to skate on. That's just amazing to me."

If there had been any real concern about the Edmonton ice makers losing their jobs, it was quickly put to rest when Trent Evans' boss back in Edmonton, Ken Knowles, told reporters that there was nothing for the men to worry about.

"We're absolutely proud of them," said Knowles. "Aside from the medals, we've got another story here that will go down in history."

The story, however, was still not through. The Salt Lake Organizing Committee – the body that had ordered the coin be removed that first week – was not at all amused. A high-ranking official put in a call to Bob Nicholson the moment he returned to the Calgary offices of the Canadian Hockey Association.

"We need the coin back," the caller stated. No reason was specified.

"I'd love to give it to you," said Nicholson. "But I don't have it. It's already gone to the Hockey Hall of Fame."

The moment Nicholson hung up, he put in a call to Bill Hay, the chair of the Hall of Fame, and warned him that he, too, was about to get a call demanding the loonie back.

"It's Canadian property," a stern-voiced Hay told the Salt Lake caller.

"And it's staying here."

In March, the coin went on display at the Hall, the centre-piece of an exhibit featuring photographs of both the men's and women's teams in the moments after they had won their gold medals.

The coin was placed in a special holder between the two blowups of the teams, with a small hole in the display just large enough to let visitors stick a finger through and briefly

touch the precious good-luck charm. They later had to cover it up; so many hockey fans wanted to touch the loonie, it was beginning to wear away.

A press release to accompany the unveiling of the new display said, "Good luck monuments have become famous in countries around the world. The Greeks built good luck hero statues of Hercules and Adonis, the Irish have the Blarney Stone and four-leaf clovers, and the Canadians have the Salt Lake Loonie. We're proud to house this good luck charm, and to give fans a chance to rub off some of its good luck."

"On the money market this loonie is worth sixty-three cents," curator Phil Pritchard told the large gathering at the display's unveiling. "To the Hall and to hockey fans, it's worth its weight in gold, twice over."

Trent Evans was there at the unveiling as well. *Twice*. Once in the photograph of the men's team, standing just over Al MacInnis' shoulder on the men's bench, waiting with his bottle of hot water and screwdriver.

And also in person, as the special guest of honour.

What, he was later asked, would he have done with the loonie if the two teams had not won the gold medals?

"Simple," he grinned. "Dug it out and taken it home – and probably used it the next morning to buy a coffee on the way in to work."

Acknowledgements

Roy MacGregor and Wayne Gretzky wish to thank Bruce Westwood of Westwood Creative Artists, who put all this together and who has graciously donated his time and agent's commission to the Wayne Gretzky Foundation. They would also like to thank Phil Taylor of the Royal Canadian Mint, Brad Pascall of the Canadian Hockey Association, Rick Minch of WDG Enterprises, and Alex Schultz of McClelland & Stewart, who was able to polish off, and polish up, everything that Bruce Westwood set in motion.